The Sisterhood

A play by
Molière

Translated and adapted by
R. R. Bolt

Samuel French – London
New York – Sydney – Toronto – Hollywood

Please see page vi for further copyright information

THE SISTERHOOD

First performed at the New End Theatre, Hampstead, London, on 3rd November, 1987, with the following cast of characters:

Armande	Jacqueline Tong
Henriette	Arabella Weir
Clitandre	Stephen May
Bélise	Lesley Joseph
Ariste	Thomas Wheatley
Chrysale	Clive Swift
Martine	Jacqueline Tong
Philaminte	Janet Henfrey
Trissotin	Thomas Wheatley
Vadius	Clive Swift

Directed by Jonathan Critchley

The action of the play takes place in Philaminte's salon in Paris

Time—the present

CHARACTERS

Philaminte, wife of Chrysale, mother of Henriette and
  Armande
Chrysale, Philaminte's husband
Henriette, daughter of Chrysale and Philaminte, in love
  with Clitandre
Bélise, Chrysale's sister
Ariste, Chrysale's brother
Clitandre, an impoverished youth of good family, in love
  with Henriette
Trissotin, a pseud
Vadius, a pseud
Martine, a servant

For Patrick Harbinson

ACT I

Philaminte's salon, Paris

Henriette and Armande

Armande If you give "Mademoiselle" up for "Madame",
　Believe me, life will never be the same.
　But do you really mean to celebrate
　Your entry into hell—I mean the state
　Of wedlock?
Henriette 　　　　I do.
Armande 　　　　　　　　"I do"—that little phrase
　Induces instantaneous malaise.
Henriette Does marriage really fill you with such dread?
Armande Shame on you!
Henriette 　　　　Pardon?
Armande 　　　　　　　　Shame on you, I said.
　"Marriage"—think back: when have you ever heard
　Such a supremely nauseating word?
　A word that made you feel so out of sorts?
　A word that conjured up such ghastly thoughts?
　Why aren't you shuddering? Do you realize
　What living torment such a word implies?
Henriette The only thoughts it conjures up for me
　Are of a husband, home and family.
　I'm sorry, but I fail to see in that
　Anything to revile, or shudder at.
　Perhaps this will surprise you, but one can
　Find happiness—*fulfilment*—with a man.
　There's such a thing as wedded bliss, you know.
Armande I'm horrified to see you've sunk this low!
　Have you so little sense of your potential
　That you believe such trivia essential?
　Does happiness mean nothing better than
　Spawning some brats and worshipping a man?
　Is that your view? Of course not—it's absurd.
　Please, leave such "pleasures" to the common herd,
　And while they wallow in them, set your sights
　On higher things and more refined delights.
　To join our sisterhood you must reject
　The sensory world and trust the intellect.
Henriette We ought to let our genes decide what's best:

People are different—some of us are blessed
With aspirations and a brilliant mind—
Others are less ... platonically inclined:
I can't reverse the accident of birth
That made you lofty, and me down-to-earth.

Armande Just look at Mother: many feel that she
Deserves a place in the Académie,
And Monsieur Trissotin is in no doubt
That anti-feminists have kept her out.
How else can either of us justify
Being *her* daughter than by aiming high?
Marriage is slavery, but it needn't be—
Not if ... literature and philosophy
Are what you marry—sociology,
Politics, semantics, semiology,
Hermeneutics, logic—disciplines like these
Won't beat you up or screw their secretaries—
These are my husbands—frankly, I'm appalled
By all this hankering after "love", so-called.

Henriette What you've described sounds like polygamy—
One flesh-and-blood husband's quite enough for me.
Why can't we both just follow Nature's law
And stick to what we've got an instinct for?
My sister may be destined for the ether—
I'm quite content to crawl along beneath her.
You seek fulfilment one way, I another,
But both of us are imitating Mother:
Her thoughts weren't always so ethereal—
"Mother" has the same root as "material"—
How do you think we got here, anyway?
At least two earthly lapses, I should say!

Armande When using someone as a model, one
Selects their strongest points to focus on:
Such an assessment of their qualities
Needn't include the way they cough and sneeze!

Henriette I think you've let your passion for aesthetics
Blind you to the importance of genetics:
Who knows what future Einstein I'll abort
If I give up sex for speculative thought?

Armande What can men offer us that we can't get
Ourselves, with more enjoyment and less sweat?
If you're in any doubt, read Andrea Dworkin—
She said it all.

Henriette   That's your frustration talking.

Armande Frustration! Men can rot, for all I care—
Castrate the lot—I wouldn't turn a hair.

Henriette A woman's independence needn't be
Impeded by her sexuality:

Just look at that Italian MP—
The one who used to be a porno star—
La Cicciolina—she didn't get that far
By burning, but by peeling off her bra!

Armande If I can't cure your mania for a mate
I trust it's not Clitandre, at any rate.

Henriette Why? What have I to be ashamed of there?

Armande That's not the point—I mean it isn't fair:
You know full well he once proposed to me.

Henriette Yes—and how stupid can a lover be?
To worship you, who openly disparage
Sex in general, and particularly marriage.
Unless it's to "philosophy", of course—
Or another of those disciplines of yours.

Armande All right, but admiration has its place:
A clever man's devotion's no disgrace.

Henriette I've never tried to stop these genuflections
At the altar of your manifold perfections—
I've simply taken what he offered me:
A loving heart that, thanks to you, was free.
And what's more, if you think I'm going to let
My husband dominate me, don't forget:
Clitandre is penniless, whereas I'm rich—
At least, I soon will be, in view of which,
If he gets difficult I'm sure a show
Of strength will soon restore the status quo.

Armande I wouldn't count on being rich—unless
Mother agrees you'll *both* be penniless.
Anyway, you're his second choice—as such,
His love for you may not amount to much.
Are you so confident that your appeal
Can help him conquer what he must still feel
For me?

Henriette I'm confident.

Armande Be careful, though—
Men can deceive them*selves* as well, you know.

Clitandre enters

Henriette (*as Clitandre enters*)
Perhaps—but here he comes—I tell you what:
Let's clarify this matter on the spot.
(*To Clitandre*) We'd like to ask you something . . .

Clitandre Please—feel free.

Henriette Who do you really love—Armande or me?

Armande Don't answer—why should we subject your passion
To all the rigours of an explanation?
I've had experience of this sort of thing—
I know it can be most embarrassing.

Clitandre I'm a simple man—I can't equivocate—
    I like to play things absolutely straight,
    So here's the truth, as plain as it can get:
    I don't love you—I do love Henriette.
    You shouldn't be distressed—I would've thought
    You half expected something of the sort.
    I loved you desperately—I made that plain—
    But not as plain as *you* made your disdain.
    You seemed intent on trampling over me—
    I offered love—you wanted slavery.
    At last I tired of it, and I decided
    To find a woman who at least abided
    By rudimentary standards of behaviour.
    You were my hell, your sister was my saviour:
    She dried my tears and tended my wounds—
    I'll never throw away this pearl I've found—
    She doesn't mind that I've been spurned by you—
    You'd be amazed what tenderness can do—
    It's no use trying to take me from her now.
Armande What makes you think I'd want to, anyhow?
    It's an impertinence to even mention
    Something of which I've not the least intention.
    Typical of a man: "I'm so damned good,
    It's me or Superman or spinsterhood!"
Henriette Armande! What's happened to that discipline
    That helps you hold your baser urges in?
    Can't it control your temper?
Armande   Henriette,
    I hope you don't imagine I'm upset.
Henriette Of course not! After all, you set no store
    By the things we lesser mortals hanker for.
    I wouldn't have the insolence to suggest
    That *you* could show the slightest interest
    In this affair of ours—although I trust
    You're going to put our case to Mother, just
    To show us how disinterested you *are*—
    Since, as you pointed out, she has the power
    To make things pretty difficult for us—
    But I'm sure this request's superfluous!
Armande Such exultation! Hard to understand
    Over a heart you've picked up second-hand.
Henriette That one again—well, second-hand or not,
    If it was free you'd take it like a shot.
Armande This sort of bickering I can't endure—
    Goodbye!

    Armande exits

Henriette (*calling after her*)

Very restrained of you, I'm sure!
(*To Clitandre*) I think your frankness caught her unawares.
Clitandre It serves her right for putting on such airs—
     She deserves everything she gets.
Henriette   Quite true.
     But look, Clitandre, there's still a lot to do:
     Unless my parents sanction it, this match
     Could well be long on love and short on cash.
     We have to work on them, without delay.
Clitandre (*going*)
     I'll go and see your father right away.
Henriette No, wait—Father's consent is quickly won,
     And seldom of much use to anyone.
     He's affable, he likes a quiet life,
     Which tends to mean kotowing to his wife.
     "What Mother says goes"—that's our household creed—
     And her consent is what we really need.
     Above all, she's the one with all the cash.
Clitandre What if she is? What's money? So much trash
     As long as I've got you.
Henriette   I'm touched, of course—
     But surely you agree, we *could* do worse
     Than have our love and lots of money too,
     Since we don't need to choose.
Clitandre   I guess that's true.
Henriette If only you could find it in your heart
     To make yourself agreeable—just start
     Flattering her a little—*and* my aunt.
Clitandre If you mean compromise myself, I can't.
     I can't abide learning for learning's sake.
     Even from *her* I found it hard to take.
     (*He points off to where Armande has just exited*)
     Don't get me wrong—I have a great respect
     For women of superior intellect—
     I don't resent their cleverness one bit,
     But why make such a song and dance of it?
     Let them know everything there is to know,
     But don't let's have it constantly on show.
     Your mother's fine—I'd love to be her son-
     In-law—but I despise her hangers-on—
     Especially the ghastly Trissotin—
     It hurts to see her worshipping that man—
     She treats him like a second Roland Barthes—
     Why can't she see he's just a bogus . . .
Henriette   Look:
     If Mother thinks that Trissotin's first rate
     Then he's the man you have to cultivate.
     The choice you've got to make is simple: me,

Or—God preserve us—your integrity.
And if it's me, you'll have to learn to please
Everybody—even her Pekinese.
Clitandre I'll go to the four corners of the globe,
But I won't praise *him*—I'm a Trissotophobe—
At least, I would, if only he'd abjure
This dreadful dabbling in literature.
He's a one-man rubbish factory, churning out
His turgid tosh and touting it about.
His writing reeks of mediocrity.
Henriette It's not exactly brilliant, I agree.
Clitandre Even before we met I felt I knew
What he'd be like from reading his reviews—
They've got a subtext that's as plain as day:
"We're written by a fool!" they seem to say—
"A posturing, pontificating prat!"
And when I *did* meet him he *was* just that—
Acting the colonel with a raw recruit—
Wigging me for forgetting to salute.
Henriette How drole.
Clitandre   I'm serious—the man's imbued
With the aura of a thoroughgoing pseud—
His bearing came as no surprise to me—
It's as portentous as his poetry.
We first met at a party, and before
They'd told me who he was, I said: "Bonjour!
Trissotin, I presume?" And sure enough
It *was* the very man—I was quite chuffed!
Henriette (*drily*)
Bravo.
Clitandre But look—here comes your aunt, on cue—
I'll start on her, if that's all right with you.
I'll tell her everything—I should've thought
We'd a good chance of gaining her support.

Bélise enters

Bélise Your mother here?
Henriette   She's due back at eleven ...
Clitandre would like a word with you.
Bélise (*suggestive*)
                              Good Heavens! (*She moves towards*
Clitandre)

Henriette exits

Clitandre Madame, I'd like a minute of your time ...
It's rather delicate ... The fact is ... I'm
Quite desperately in love with ...
Bélise   Please, no more:

This openness is something I deplore
In lovers—I shall add you to my list—
But if I do, I really must insist
On more discretion—you should be content
With the occasional acknowledgement.
Likewise, on your side, looks and signs will do—
Anything more, and I've no room for you.
Clitandre Oh, don't have any worries on that score—
Henriette is the woman I adore:
Love you! Good Lord, no! Nothing of the sort—
I don't want love from you, I want support.
Bélise I see! You've found your heart an alibi—
You're trying to put me off the scent: nice try!
Well, I've got nothing against undercover
Wooing—in fact, one likes to see a lover
Showing a bit of ingenuity—
Laclos's my favourite novelist.
Clitandre (*dismissively*)
                                   Is he?
Well, ingenuity's just not my line—
You couldn't find a franker tongue than mine.
I really mean to marry Henriette,
But I need all the assistance I can get.
You see . . .
Bélise   Let's talk in code—that's fine by me:
Well then—I'm Henriette—now, let me see:
(*making quotation marks in the air*)
"Henriette", I fear, is not the marrying kind—
You won't get far if you have *that* in mind!
Clitandre For Christ's sake, what's the point of this charade?
Bélise Come on! You're making this extremely hard:
Don't be ashamed—this method of revealing
Your love for me is novel and appealing.
But I can't say it's come as a surprise:
D'you think I haven't seen it in your eyes?
Those tell-tale glances that, for some time now,
You've thrown my way? Well then, if this is how
You choose to verbalize your feelings, I
Have no objection—love on.
Clitandre   But . . .
Bélise   Goodbye.
I've already said more than I meant to say.
Clitandre But look . . .
Bélise   I'm blushing . . .
Clitandre   Let's put it this way:
I'll be hanged if I'm in love with you—how's that?
Bélise (*aside*)
He's quite bewitched!

Clitandre (*aside, exasperated*)
                       What *is* she playing at?!
Bélise (*aside*)
I'm always having this effect on men!
(*To Clitandre*) Come round this evening—we'll discuss it then.

Bélise exits

Clitandre Her life's a vast, Priapic fantasy—
Perhaps she's just discovered LSD.
She's half Caligula, half Erica Jong—
She wishes mankind had a single dong!
I need help—but now her appetite's been whetted
Heaven knows what I'll have to do to get it!

Black-out

ACT II

The same

Ariste and Clitandre

Ariste I do have influence, in my own small way—
  I lunched with Raymond Barre the other day—
  He's trying to reorganize the Right
  And he wants men like you to join the fight:
  Unless I read the signs completely wrong
  You're sure to get the call before too long.
Clitandre How can I thank you? But ... you won't forget
  That other matter?
Ariste   You mean Henriette?
  I'll put your case as strongly as I can,
  And then report straight back. Relax!

  Clitandre exits

                    Poor man!
  The lengths some lovers go to are absurd—
  This endless talk, for what? One measly word.

  Chrysale enters

  Hello there, brother! How are things with you?
Chrysale Not bad.
Ariste   Good! SPLENDID!! (*He slaps him on the back*)
Chrysale   What's this leading to?
Ariste Clitandre—you've known him for a few years now?
Chrysale Since he was so high.
Ariste   Is that so? And how
  D'you rate him?
Chrysale   Oh, first-class—straight as a die—
  You couldn't hope to meet a nicer guy.
Ariste I'm glad you think so.
Chrysale   Yes—I knew his father—
  We spent a holiday in Rome together.
Ariste Oh?
Chrysale Hmm. He was a first-rate chap as well:
  We were twenty-eight, and fond of raising hell.
  We showed those Roman girls a thing or two—
  We broke some hearts ...

Ariste   I'd expect that from you.
  Well—let me tell you what I came here for:

Bélise enters

  Clitandre has made me his ambassador:
  The fact is, he's in love with Henriette—
  As deep in love as anyone can get.
Chrysale He loves my daughter?
Bélise   No. You're quite wrong there.
Ariste ⎫ (*together*) What?
Chrysale ⎭
Bélise   I can shed some light on this affair.
  Somebody's had a joke at your expense—
  Clitandre's in love—but not with her.
Ariste   Nonsense!
  He told me . . .
Bélise Oh, indeed?
Ariste   He sent me here,
  Because he knew I had her father's ear,
  To put his case.
Bélise   Excellent! Very neat!
  A gallant and ingenious counterfeit!
  He really is a chip off the old block—
  His methods have a touch of the Baroque.
  But, brothers, I can disabuse you both.
Ariste What do you know about it?
Bélise   Just the truth.
  He really loves . . .
Chrysale   Yes?
Bélise   Me.
Ariste ⎫ (*together*)   YOU!!!
Chrysale ⎭
Bélise   Yes.
Ariste ⎫ (*together*)   WHO???
Chrysale ⎭
Bélise   Me.
Chrysale I don't believe it!
Bélise   Why not?
Ariste   Seriously?
Bélise It's hardly flattering, all this stupefaction—
  Men aren't exactly blind to my attractions!
Chrysale What men?
Bélise   Lycas, Dorante, Cléonte, Damis . . .
Ariste They all love you?
Bélise   All of them—frantically.
Chrysale They've told you so?
Bélise   Oh, no, they wouldn't dare—
  Their reverence won't permit them to declare

Their love—they render me their services
With little tokens, silent offices.
Ariste Damis is hardly ever here these days.
Bélise That only shows how meekly he obeys.
Chrysale Dorante maligns you quite outrageously.
Bélise Of course he does—he's mad with jealousy.
Ariste The other two, as far as I'm aware,
  Have got engaged.
Bélise   Yes. Out of sheer despair.
Ariste I must say, you're a vivid fantasist.
Chrysale A vision worthy of the Evangelist!
Bélise Evangelist, indeed! Well, I must say,
  I *have* heard some amusing things today.
  I always knew I was a woman of vision,
  And now, at last, I get some recognition!

Bélise exits

Chrysale Our sister's going balmy!
Ariste   Going? Gone!
  It's getting worse, too! But let's carry on
  With our discussion, and Clitandre's suit—
  What kind of answer are you planning to it?
Chrysale What answer *could* there be, but to rejoice?
  I'm thrilled, not to say honoured, by his choice.
Ariste Of course, you know he's not exactly rich?
Chrysale But he has many virtues, each of which
  Is worth a mint—*his father's an old friend.*
Ariste Good. That just leaves your wife. With her in mind . . .
Chrysale Why bother her? I've agreed, haven't I?
Ariste But why not, as one might say, *ratify*
  Your own approval by obtaining hers?
Chrysale That would be utterly superfluous:
  I'm taking full responsibility.
Ariste Yeeees, but I'd rather . . .
Chrysale   Please, leave this to me.
Ariste I'll talk to Henriette, and then we'll see . . .
Chrysale See what?
Ariste   Nothing.
Chrysale   It's a *fait accompli.*
  I'll tell my wife about it rightaway.

Martine enters

Martine Bloody 'ek! Don't never be no-one's servant—that's what I say!
  Why is a servant like a puppy-dog?
  If you don' wannit you pretend it's got rabies and flush it down the bog!
Ariste She seems upset.
Chrysale (*to Martine*)
                     Now, what's this all about?

Ariste I think I'll leave you two to sort it out.

Ariste exits

Chrysale Martine, what's up?
Martine   What's up 'e says! I've just got the sack.
Chrysale What for?
Martine 'Ow should I know? Just get that bloody wife er yours off my back.
Chrysale You're a good girl—I'm very pleased with you—
Leave this to me—I'll see what I can do.
My wife's quite ... temperamental, I'm afraid.
Martine You're telling me!

Philaminte and Bélise enter

Philaminte Ah! There's that wretched maid.
(*To Martine*) Out of my house at once! Get out, I say!
Chrysale Steady!
Philaminte (*to Chrysale*)
                          It's no use—I've dismissed her.
Chrysale   Hey!
Hang on a minute—what's she done to ... ?
Philaminte   What?!
If this means you're supporting her ...
Chrysale   I'm not—
But there must be a reason ...
Philaminte   That'll do.
Why should I justify myself to you?
I *have* my reasons.
Chrysale   Well, I'd like to know ...
Philaminte I'm adamant—Martine has got to go.
Chrysale And I've said nothing to the contrary!
Philaminte I won't have anyone obstructing me.
Chrysale All right.
Bélise   And what's more, if you were a good
Husband you'd take her side, as husbands should.
Chrysale (*to Martine*)
My wife's quite right—she's scolded you before—
But this is absolutely the last straw—
It's unforgivable! Get out of here!
Martine What've I *done*, monsieur?
Chrysale   I've no idea!
Philaminte The girl's too thick to see how serious
Her failings are—there's nothing to discuss.
Chrysale BUT WHAT'S SHE DONE? Broken some pan or pot?
Put china in the dishwasher, or what?
Philaminte That's not the sort of thing I'd sack her for.
I'm not a maniac.
Chrysale   So it's a more
Important matter ... (*He thinks*)

Philaminte   Look, don't play the fool—
It takes a lot to make me lose my cool.
Chrysale Did she forget to lock the doors last night?
Have we been burgled?
Philaminte   Oh, no, it's a sight
More serious than that.
Chrysale   You caught her stealing?!
Bélise Goodness! What bourgeois values we're revealing!
Chrysale My God! I think I've got it—you don't mean
Her boyfriend spent the night here? It's obscene!!
Bélise Her crime's the worst a human can commit:
She's an ignorant, illiterate half-wit.
Philaminte I've tried to teach her, but she's beaten me:
She's got the syntax of a child of three.
Chrysale Is that all?
Philaminte   ALL?! To undermine the very
Foundations of all rational enquiry?
Bélise To break the laws that govern everyone
From down-and-outs to François Mitterand?
Chrysale I thought she'd done something a little more ...
Meaty—if that's the word.
Philaminte   I take it you're
Defending her?
Chrysale   God, no!
Philaminte   Please—if you want
To put her case, feel free.
Chrysale   I don't! I can't!
Bélise Her speech is an apology for French —
It's garbage—you can almost smell the stench!
Martine I know I don' talk proper, 'n I 'umbly beg yer pardon,
But I can't make 'ead or tail er your soddin' jargon.
You can go in for all that fancy talk if you like but I'm definitely not
Gonna decompose.
Bélise   It's "DECONSTRUCT," you clot!
Philaminte Jargon she calls it!
Martine   Yeah. 'Cos talk's no good,
No matter 'ow clever it is, if it can' even be understood.
Philaminte She hasn't shown the slightest inclination
To get herself a decent education:
To think of all the hours I've spent with her,
Examining Saussure and Derrida!
I've laboured day and night—I've tried and tried—
She still confuses sign with signified.
Bélise She failed on generative grammar, too.
Martine I would'n drag my grandma into this if yer know what's good for
you!
Bélise Ge-ner-at-ive gram-mar! Chomsky!
Martine   You what?

Bélise This girl is a congenital idiot.
Martine Don' you dare use filthy language like that with me!
Bélise Utter, mindboggling stupidity!
    No, if you're teaching her you needn't look
    Beyond some crayons and a colouring book.
Philaminte So, are we getting rid of her or not?
Chrysale (*to Martine*)
    I'm sorry—I don't see what choice I've got.
    I promise you, you'll get a first-class reference.
Philaminte How can you treat this moron with such deference?
Chrysale Who? Me? Heaven forbid! (*Turning on Martine*) Be off with you!
    (*Sotto voce*) Come back later—I'll see what I can do.

    Martine exits, kissing Chrysale as she goes

    There now, she's gone—I hope you're satisfied.
    Don't say I sanctioned it—I'm on her side
    She did what she was told and did it well—
    That was her crime, as far as I can tell.
    If you ask me, it's terribly unfair!
Philaminte I'm sorry, but she drove me to despair:
    Her idiocy was addling my brain—
    Her talk reminds me of a blocked-up drain:
    Filthy and futile—just a raucous din,
    With the odd little homespun truth thrown in.
Bélise We read some Mallarmé the other day—
    I was appalled—you should have heard the way
    She lumbered through those delicate quatrains—
    It caused me genuine physical pain!
Chrysale She may be baffled by some stupid book,
    But she's a good servant, and a first-rate cook.
    Her intellect's of no concern to me,
    If she can do my gigot to a T
    And season it with the appropriate herbs.
    I don't eat adjectives, I don't drink verbs—
    Chomsky may know the origins of grammar,
    But can he crack an egg without a hammer?
Philaminte God! What a typically masculine attitude:
    "To Hell with civilization—where's my food?"
    Mind/body problems don't apply to you:
    You're just unthinking body, through and through.
    The plain man's answer to the *Cogito*:
    "I eat and drink, therefore I am."
Chrysale   Quite so:
    One's body grows on one, as you might say—
    I'm getting more attached to mine each day.
Bélise I must say, it distresses me to find
    Your stomach lording it over your mind.
    Haven't you ever heard of spiritual food?

Chrysale Certainly, and I'm told it's not much good:
I like to eat ...
Philaminte   We know you like to eat—
One only has to look at you to see it.
Chrysale Now listen here! I've had enough of this:
I've held this in for years, but here it is—
The awful truth: EVERYONE LAUGHS AT YOU!
Philaminte (*looking round*)
I'm sorry?
Chrysale   Yes, it's you I'm talking to.
So quick to criticize, you fail to see
The full extent of your own lunacy.
If I were you, I'd burn these books of yours
(Except that set of Molières, of course—
They're worth a fortune) and I don't much care
For those outrageous spectacles you wear.
You've got things all mixed-up—your *rôle* in life
Should not be that of professeuse, but wife:
Why waste your time with all this bogus stuff?
As if running a household weren't enough.
A woman's proper place is in the home—
And not knee-deep in some portentous tome.
Once upon a time, no female dreamed of knowing
About anything but cookery and sewing.
Those were the days! That was the Golden Age—
A woman never read or wrote a page—
Her only library was a sewing box—
Her special subjects? Crochet, nappies, frocks.
But that's not good enough for you—your calling
Is to be Proust, Déscartes and Pascal, all in
One. You're forever wallowing in knowledge—
This used to be a home—now it's a college:
The servants don't do what they're meant to do—
Half the time they're in seminars with you:
"Don't ask the maid to sew that button on—
She's writing an essay on de Maupassant."
"Sorry—the chauffeur's occupied today:
He's comparing Baudelaire with Mallarmé!"
I haven't even mentioned your worst sin—
Your friendship with the ghastly Trissotin.
Bélise To think such bourgeois sentiments could spring
From one's own flesh and blood! It's sickening.
You know, we occupied the self-same womb!
I'm sorry—I shall have to leave the room!

Bélise exits

Philaminte Well, what a devastating exposé!
Do carry on ...

Chrysale　　　I've nothing more to say
On that score, but there's something else we've got
To talk about: our eldest daughter's not—
She's never going to be—the marrying kind,
But Henriette's quite differently inclined—
I think it's time ...
Philaminte　　　You must have read my mind!
What's more, I think I've found the very man.
Chrysale Who's that?
Philaminte　　　Guess.
Chrysale　　　Not ... ?
Philaminte　　　Well?
Chrysale　　　No!
Philaminte　　　Yes—Trissotin.
He's *my* first choice, although he doesn't seem
To have exactly soared in *your* esteem.
I think he'd make the perfect son-in-law—
I'm the best judge in these affairs—what's more
I'm not prepared to argue with you, so
DON'T TRY TO INTERFERE—I'm sure to know
If you do.

Philaminte exits and Ariste enters

Ariste How'd it go?
Chrysale　　　Not brilliantly.
Ariste Was she against it?
Chrysale　　　Not specifically.
Ariste She's undecided?
Chrysale　　　No. That's not it either—
She's picked a different person altogether.
Ariste What's his name? Spit it out!
Chrysale　　　Trissotin.
Ariste　　　WHAT???!!!
Chrysale Tris-so-tin!
Ariste　　　No! That meretricious twot?!
And what was your response?
Chrysale　　　I held my peace.
Ariste You didn't even put Clitandre's case?
Chrysale No—when I saw which way the wind was blowing
I beat a tactical retreat.
Ariste　　　Nice going!
A bashful virgin wouldn't be so meek—
You're like a cup of bad tea— wet and weak.
You should be on show: "the man without a spine"!
Chrysale OK, but you're not in the firing line.
Just look at me: a gentle, placid man
Married to a rampaging hooligan;
She may be a philosopher and scholar—

She's also a volcanic mass of choler.
For each objection I might raise to *her* wishes
I'd get involved in countless bruising skirmishes—
So when she's frothing at the mouth and snarling
I force myself to call her "dear" and "darling".

Ariste Oh, not—don't put the cart before the horse:
It's my belief you've made things ten times worse
By giving in to her at every turn—
Watching responses is the way we learn
How to behave—or misbehave: why not,
This once, at least, try telling *her* what's what?
Convince a doubting world you're still a man—
Say "THIS IS WHAT I WANT" if you still can.

Chrysale You're right—I'll brace myself for an assault.

Ariste That's it!

Chrysale I've acted like an utter dolt.

Ariste Well said.

Chrysale   She takes my temperament for granted—
Exploits my gentleness. . . .

Ariste   This is what's wanted.

Chrysale It's time for action . . .

There is an embarrassing pause, as Chrysale tries to decide on something

                              . . . go and find Clitandre
   And send him here.

Ariste   Your wish is my command.

   Ariste exits

Chrysale I've had about as much as I can take—
My very sexuality's at stake!

Black-out

ACT III

The same

Philaminte, Armande, and Bélise

Philaminte This afternoon I'd like us all to listen
  To a poem Monsieur Trissotin's just written.
  He's in my study polishing it now.
Armande That man's phenomenal.
Bélise   I don't know how
  He does it.
Philaminte   Speed and talent often go
  Together—look at Shakespeare—Mozart ...
Bélise   Though
  Flaubert wrote half a paragraph a night,
  And Virgil did two lines a day, and ...
Philaminte   Quite.

Pause

Armande I'm all a-flutter with anticipation!
Bélise His every word excites one's admiration.
Armande As far as *poets* go, he has no peer.
Bélise To get that sort of pleasure through one's ear!

  Henriette enters, sees the gathering and ...

Henriette Oh. (*She attempts to leave*)
Philaminte Henriette! Don't scuttle off! COME HERE!!
Henriette It's all right—I don't want to interfere.
Bélise We're going to hear some verse, fresh from the pen
  Of one of France's most creative men!
Henriette It's not my province.
Philaminte   Be that as it may,
  We need to talk—I ORDER YOU TO STAY.

  *Trissotin now makes a triumphant entrance, brandishing the manuscript of
  his new poem*

Philaminte Ah, Trissotin! We're in an agony
  Of expectation.
Trissotin   Please—you flatter me.
Philaminte Is it a haiku or an epigram?
Trissotin It's a new-born child—your ears will be its pram.

In fact, you're its godmother, so to speak—
I conceived it in your lavabo last week.
Bélise He's brilliant!

Trissotin is ogling Henriette, who rises and again attempts to leave

Henriette Look, I really fail to see
What this distinguished gathering wants with me.
Philaminte You'll find out soon enough.
Bélise   I've never known
Such stubbornness!
Armande   Henriette, please sit down.
Bélise You're ruining a feast of poetry.
Henriette What if I'm not that hungry?
Trissotin   Let her be—
To tax her mind would only do her harm,
And militate against her natural charm.
Henriette (*not having this*)
I'll stay.
Philaminte Let's have the new-born child!
Bélise   The feast!
Trissotin A hunger such as yours will need at least
One piece to satisfy it, so I'll start
With another little sample of my art—
I hope I'm not being boastful if I say
It's quite amusing, in its own small way—
It's earned some praise . . .
Bélise   I'm sure it has . . .
Philaminte   We're waiting . . .
Bélise (*interrupting Trissotin three times as he attempts to read*)
I'm so worked up I'm almost palpitating!
Poetry has a strange effect on me . . .
Especially erotic poetry.
Philaminte Contain yourself—we haven't heard it yet.

Trissotin again attempts to read, but is now interrupted by Henriette sneezing

Henriette Atchoo! Atchoo!
Bélise   Be quiet, Henriette!
Trissotin (*reading*)
          "Sonnet to a Princess Suffering from a Viral Infection"

                    "It's utter lunacy
                    To harbour in your mind
                    Blowing body this kind
                    Of deadly enemy."

Bélise What a beginning!
Armande   I can hardly speak!
Bélise (*with a hint of obscenity*)
He really has an excellent technique!

Armande That opening line! "It's utter lunacy . . ."
  So . . . poignant.
Philaminte   Harbouring one's enemy—
  A lovely paradox.
Bélise   Juxtaposition—
  One of the hallmarks of a skilled technician.
Philaminte Let's hear the rest.
Trissotin (*reading*)

> "It's utter lunacy
> To harbour in your mind
> blowing body this kind
> Of deadly enemy."

Bélise ⎫
Armande ⎰ (*together*) Stunning!
Philaminte   First-rate!
Trissotin (*reading*)

> "Evict it now, I say!
> It's squatting (can't you see it?)
> In your body's penthouse suite,
> Eating your life away!"

Bélise I feel quite faint! Stop reading for a bit.
Armande We need a moment to examine it.
Bélise There's something in the way the words combine
  That sends a shiver running down my spine.

Armande   "Evict it now, I say!
          It's squatting (can't you see it?)"

What's next? Yes—"In your body's penthouse suite"—
The metaphor's particularly neat.
Philaminte (*to Trissotin*)
  What I like is the way that you extend
  That metaphor right to its bitter end.
Armande Yes, that's the point: "Evict it now, I say!"
Bélise He slips it in in such a nimble way!
Armande I wish I'd written it.
Bélise   To *be* that good!
Philaminte I wonder if you've fully understood . . .
Armande ⎫
Bélise ⎰ (*together*) Oh, please!
Philaminte   "Evict it now" and "penthouse suite" . . .
  The subtext is political—the élite
  Against the proletariate—a class war
  Fought in a woman's body.
Bélise   Yes! The more
  One teases it, the more one winkles out!

Philaminte Class as contagion—that's what it's about.
   You follow?
Armande Every word is charged with meaning.
Bélise It's educational *and* entertaining.
Philaminte Indeed it is. (*To Trissotin*) I have a question, though:
   When you composed the poem, did you know
   What you were doing? Did you have in mind
   The dialectic that I've just defined?
Trissotin Of course.
Armande   The image of a squat agrees
   So well with *my* conception of disease:
   Your body is its shelter, and in lieu
   Of thanks it makes a total mess of you!
Philaminte In summary, two excellent quatrains.
Armande I wouldn't mind that second one again.
Trissotin (*reading*)

> "Evict it now, I say!
> It's squatting (can't you see it?)
> In your body's penthouse suite,
> Eating your life away!"

Bélise ⎫
Armande ⎭ (*together*) Superb!
Philaminte   Quiet!
Trissotin (*reading*)

> "Your status does no good—
> It lurks in your blue blood
> Harming you day and night.
> A trip to Lourdes might do
> The trick—the waters might
> Drown it, before *it* drowns *you*!"

Philaminte Perfect.
Bélise My brain is in a whirl!
Armande   So's mine!
Philaminte I can't remember anything so fine.
   Your work's a garden—everywhere one goes
   One stoops to pluck a perfect verbal rose!
Trissotin You liked it, then?
Philaminte   Liked it! It dazzled me!
Armande Such talent! Such originality!
Bélise (*to Henriette*)
   What about you? What have you got to say?
Henriette Everyone must react in their own way.
Trissotin It didn't shock you?
Henriette   No—I wasn't listening.
Philaminte It's time that new-born baby got its christening.

Trissotin (*producing another poem from about his person; reading*)
"On a Purple Porsche Given to His Girlfriend".
Bélise You know, I think I like the titles best.
Armande They really make you want to hear the rest.
Trissotin (*reading*)

<blockquote>

"On a Purple Porsche Given to His Girlfriend"

"The pangs of lôve have cost me dear—
Witness this costly sportscar here—
The envy of my girlfriend's friends
As in it on her way she wends:
Call it purple, call it mauve—
I call it the price of lôve."

</blockquote>

Bélise Orgasmic!
Armande   Ravishing!
Bélise   What can one say?
  You're the foremost French poet of your day.
Philaminte There's more to *that* short text than meets the eye.
Trissotin (*a little fed up*)
  Is there, indeed?
Philaminte Of course. Now, let's just try . . .

She tries to take the poem but Trissotin puts it away

Trissotin I wish you'd let me see some verse of yours–
  I could return this generous applause.
Philaminte I don't write poems, but I'll let you look
  At the first chapter of my latest book—
  A counterblast against male domination—
  It's going to be the strongest affirmation
  Of radical feminist principles to date—
  I'm calling it *Towards a Feminist State*.
  Although, of course, the argument goes back
  To Plato, *his* remarks on women lack
  Coherence—what I'm really trying to do,
  In fact, is carry *The Republic* to
  Its logical conclusion.
Armande   True, we've made
  Enormous strides during the last decade,
  But most men, in their heart of hearts, still think
  A woman's place is at the kitchen sink.
Bélise Our chains are looser than they used to be,
  But they haven't snapped—we haven't broken free.
Trissotin I've always been a champion of your cause—
  Although, as man and poet, one adores
  A woman's body, one can also find
  A lot to occupy one in her mind.
Philaminte You're an honorary woman—you know that;

You're not the kind of man we're aiming at—
A lot of "intellectuals" don't respect,
Or even acknowledge, female intellect.
The work we're doing's revolutionary—
Genuinely interdisciplinary—
A blend of politics, biology,
Logic, semantics, sociology . . .

Bélise Give me Derrida's *displacement* any day.

Philaminte I still think Barthes has got a lot to say.

Trissotin When it comes to *bricolage*, Foucault's the man.

Philaminte For deconstruction no-one beats Lacan.

Bélise Perhaps. Derrida's more my cup of tea.

Trissotin Derrida's seminal, I quite agree.

Bélise I think catastrophe theory's rather neat.

Armande I love those three-D graphs!

Bélise   Yes, *aren't* they sweet?!

Armande The law of entropy could change the world.

Philaminte It does that all the time, you silly girl!

Armande Exciting content isn't all we seek—
Form matters, too—I mean the way we speak:
We're going to launch a clean-up-French campaign,
Before it goes completely down the drain.
We're still besieged by Franglais—not to mention
The home-grown faults that cry out for attention.

Philaminte Look at the way the media talk these days:
Broadcasters sound like jumped-up barrow boys
And journalists don't think their day's complete
Unless they've coined some horrible conceit.

Trissotin You're taking on a lot—I'm most impressed, though.

Bélise We ought to let him see our manifesto.

Trissotin Please do—I'm sure it's well worth looking at.

Armande Oh, no—it's worth a great deal more than that—
Time will decide—you mark my words, we'll be as
Important in the history of ideas
As Plato, or Pascal.

Trissotin   I wish you well
In your endeavours.

Bélise   Did I hear the bell?

Trissotin It's probably my friend Vadius—I took
The liberty of asking him to look
In on us here this afternoon—he's dying
To meet you all.

Philaminte   Then how can we deny him?
Credentials?

Trissotin   Top in Classics in his year
At the Ecole Normale Supérieur
Need I say more?

Bélise   Is he good-looking, though?

Trissotin Not very.
Bélise (*looking at her watch*)
      How time flies! I have to go—
I'm due to meet an artist friend at two—
Off to the Pollocks at the Pompidou.
(*To Trissotin, with grotesque coyness*) Goodbye, monsieur, or rather *au*
 revoir—
I'd forgotten just how talented you are.

Bélise exits

Philaminte Well, now . . . where are you going, Henriette?
I need to talk to you—you can't go yet.

Vadius enters

Trissotin (*drawing an initially shy Vadius forward*)
Madame Philaminte, I'm proud to introduce
One of our foremost classicists, Vadius.
Philaminte (*taking Vadius's hand*)
I'm honoured.
Vadius   NO! The honour's mine, madame.
Philaminte You won't believe how overawed I am
By people who can master ancient Greek.
Trissotin He's shown me his translations—they're unique!
Philaminte (*to Vadius*)
Allow me to embrace you—as a kind
Of tribute, if you like, to the Greek mind.

Vadius embraces her and Armande enthusiastically. He then attempts to
embrace Henriette, who emphatically declines

Henriette I'm no Hellenophile.
Philaminte   It seems to me
The Greeks were crucial, and philosophy
Is nothing but a commentary on Plato.
Vadius Ladies I trust my coming here today to
Pay homage to your brilliance doesn't cause
Undue embarrassment . . .
Philaminte   A gift like yours
Is an intellectual passe-partout.
Vadius   I'd hate
To think I'd interrupted some debate.
Trissotin He's published books, and he's a poet too.
If he's got one on him, he might show it you.
Vadius Writers these days are often plagued, I've found,
With the desire to tout their work around:
This city is awash with verse and prose—
It's an epidemic—everywhere one goes—
Street cafés, métro stations, cocktail parties,

One's mugged by ruthless gangs of arty-farties!
It's going on all over the Left Bank,
Like an enormous intellectual . . .
Trissotin   Quite.
Vadius Personally, I tend to share the view
Expressed by Horace: authors oughtn't to
Expose their works until they've left them for
Nine years to mellow in a bottom draw.
If Trissotin insists, though, I can show him
One of my latest—an erotic poem.

He hands Trissotin a manuscript which the latter takes, but shows no sign of wanting to read

Trissotin Your stuff's superb—so taut, so disciplined!
Vadius I still think yours is somehow more . . . refined.
Trissotin Your images—so accurate! So . . . true!
Vadius Ah, but for pathos there's no touching *you.*
Trissotin If genius was acknowledged, you'd have got
The Légion d'honneur years ago.
Vadius   Then what
Would *you* have got? They'd have to name some streets
Or a métro station after you, at least.
Trissotin You know a poem called "To a Princess
Suffering from a Viral Inf——
Vadius (*interrupting*)
                                          Why, yes—
Somebody read it to me yesterday—
I haven't met the author, but I'll say
This much about him, flattery apart,
His work contains more idiocy than art.
Trissotin It *has* been much admired in . . . (*he looks about him meaningfully*)
certain quarters.
Vadius The things he does to words! Lambs to the slaughter!
Trissotin I'm very sorry, but I can't agree.
Vadius They won't get tripe like that from you and me.
Trissotin In my opinion, though, for what it's worth,
There aren't too many poets on this earth
Who can write verse like that.
Vadius   I'm very glad
To hear it—if I wrote a piece that bad
I'd shoot myself!
Trissotin   You might just like to know
The perpetrator of this "piece" you're so
Dismissive of: it was me.
Vadius   Come again?
Trissotin I WAS THE ONE WHO WROTE THAT SONNET!
Vadius   When?
If it's a piece of juvenilia . . .

Trissotin   No—
  I finished it about a month ago.
Vadius I . . . can't have listened carefully enough.
  But take a look at mine—it's punchy stuff—
  Surrealist in flavour, I should say.
Trissotin I fear Surrealism's had its day.
Vadius It's hardly new—it's got a following, though.
Trissotin I think it stinks, if you really want to know. (*He hands the poem back*)
Vadius That's reassuring, coming from a hack.
Trissotin Talk about the pot calling the kettle black!
Vadius "Poets" like you deserve a prison cell.
Trissotin They could read *your* verse to punish souls in hell.
Vadius Your last book was demolished on TV.
Trissotin At least they *bother* to demolish *me*.
Vadius You're like a braggart in a Roman farce.
Trissotin You can stuff your wretched Classics up your arse!
Philaminte Gentlemen, please! What *is* this all about?
Vadius (*to Trissotin*)
  I'm off. It won't take long to sort you out—
  I'll parody your piffle to perfection!

    Vadius exits

Trissotin (*calling after him*)
  Just wait till I review your next collection!
  (*To Philaminte*) I lost my temper. I hope you weren't offended—
  I felt *your* judgement had to be defended.
Philaminte I'm going to try and sort this quarrel out.
  But first we've something else to talk about—
  Henriette, come here. (*To Henriette*) Your want of intellect
  Has always been a matter for regret
  To me. But now, with luck, I think I might
  Have found a way to help you see the light.
Henriette I'm very mediocre, I admit—
  It's no use trying to train me out of it.
  Talent looks pretty hazardous to me—
  I'll settle for a safe stupidity.
Philaminte I'm sure a safe stupidity's just fine—
  But I can't allow it in a child of mine.
  Beauty, as Horace says, is a mere flower—
  A fragile product of the fleeting hour—
  But intellectual prowess lasts forever—
  Being ugly doesn't matter if you're clever.
  What better way to understand this than
  Through friendship with a truly brilliant man?
  And who more brilliant than Trissotin?
Henriette What do you mean by "friendship"?

Philaminte   That depends—
  Husbands and wives are often just good friends.
Henriette ME marry HIM!
Trissotin   Your daughter's quite a catch.
Henriette I wouldn't count your chickens till they've hatched.
Philaminte I'll make them hatch, young lady, don't you worry—
  Girls will be girls, and I'm in no great hurry.

Philaminte exits, followed by Trissotin

Armande You've always been her favourite: Trissotin!
  He *could* be the most eligible man
  In Paris.
Henriette Do you think so? Have him, then.
Armande If he were free . . .
Henriette   He is.
Armande   But there again,
  As you observed, I openly disparage
  All human failings, and above all marriage.
Henriette I don't see why you can't extend your yen
  For intellect to intellectual men.
Armande It's Mother's wish—you have an obligation
  To give it serious consideration.

Chrysale, Ariste and Clitandre enter

Chrysale There you are, Henriette—give me your hand.

Henriette holds out her hand, which Chrysale takes and thrusts unceremoniously into Clitandre's

  Now, listen: as your father I demand . . .
  I thought perhaps you might just see your way
  To marrying Clitandre—what do you say?

Henriette embraces him, then turns to Armande with an ironic shrug

Henriette It's Father's wish—I have an obligation
  To give it serious consideration!
Armande How dare you . . .
Chrysale   Shut up! Go and find your mother—
  You can read philosophy to one another.
  Tell her what's been decided—make it clear:
  ON NO ACCOUNT IS SHE TO INTERFERE.
Clitandre I can't believe it's really happening!
Chrysale Shut up! . . . and kiss her.

Henriette and Clitandre embrace

                            Ah! This sort of thing
  Takes me right back to when I was a lad—
  It makes me weep to think what fun I had!

Chrysale wanders off, shaking his head nostalgically, as the lovers continue their embrace

Black-out

ACT IV

The same

Armande and Philaminte

Armande She did—without the slightest hesitation—
Pretended it was "filial obligation"
For ghastliness that pair are hard to beat—
Sniffing each other like two dogs on heat.
Philaminte Well, I'm not finished yet—I'll make her see
That if father and mother can't agree
Her first allegiance should be to the latter,
And mind must always triumph over matter.

Clitandre enters, realizes he is being discussed and stands to one side

Armande But what a dolt Clitandre must take you for—
To think you'd want *him* for a son-in-law!
I mean, he's nothing but a crawler, bent
On clawing his way up through government.
Philaminte I hate to disappoint him! Oh, it's true
I didn't mind when he was after you—
At least he's quite good-looking—but the rest
Of him leaves me distinctly unimpressed:
He knows I write, and yet I've never heard
Anything to suggest he's read a word.
Armande Frankly, if I were you I'd never let
A man like that run off with Henriette
People may say it's malice on my part—
Not reason talking, but a broken heart—
If so, they'd be mistaken—lesser lights
Might well be wounded by such trivial slights—
I'm armed against them with philosophy—
It's the affront to *you* that angers me.
When I think back on it, I can't recall
His ever speaking well of you at all.
Philaminte Cretin!
Armande   When critics eagerly extolled
Your work, his own reaction was ice-cold.
Philaminte Moron!
Armande   I used to read him things of yours
Anonymously—and to no applause.

Philaminte Philistine!

Clitandre (*stepping forward; addressing Armande*)
                                    Wait! Let's have some charity!
  Or failing that, a little honesty!
  (*To Philaminte*) Madame, now that you've heard the charges, I'll
  Try to defend myself, since I'm on trial.
  (*To Armande*) What damage have I done you—what offence
  Has triggered off this poisonous eloquence?

Armande I'm not offended—but suppose I was—
  Could you pretend I didn't have just cause?
  Didn't you drop me like a hot potato
  When I'd succumbed? What have you got to say to
  That? Is deceit the privilege of men?

Clitandre Well, if we must go over this again:
  My conduct was completely justified
  By your, at times, quite stupefying pride:
  Faced with that raging flood, my love was like
  A finger in an unresponsive dyke!
  You drove me off—I didn't run away—
  Why scorn me if you wanted me to stay?

Armande Scorn you! What rubbish! No—I simply tried
  To rid your love of its . . . plebeian side—
  Your passion was overtly physical—
  I didn't want that type of thing at all.
  Suppose I'd married you? What sort of life
  Would I have had as a careerist's wife?
  Stuck with some whining infant on my lap
  By day—by night, providing sex on tap.
  I had to force you to appreciate
  Me as a thinking woman, not a mate—
  I wanted to reform you—don't you see?

Clitandre Oh, yes, I understand you perfectly.
  The fact is, I'm defective—unlike you,
  I'm not all mind—I've got a body too!
  It's not a thing I'm proud of—not one bit—
  But all the same, I can't get rid of it.
  I wish I had the mental tools to sever
  Body and soul—I'm simply not that clever.
  And it's the same with girls—I seem to fall
  In love with the ensemble—body and all.
  You must admit, though, it's a common fault—
  I hardly think it warrants this assault.

Armande (*suddenly relenting*)
  I may have asked too much—perhaps you're right—
  A man can't help his sexual appetite—
  Suppose I were to take you as you are,
  Body and all—how would that be?

Clitandre   It's far

Too late for that—how could I possibly
Reject the girl whose love has set me free
And, having done so, cheerfully go back
To *you*—the one who put me on the rack?
Philaminte A noble sentiment, but you forget
That I have other plans for Henriette.
Clitandre Madame, I hope at least you'll honour me
By finding a more daunting adversary
Than Trissotin—this country is awash
With men who make their names by writing trash—
To claw one's way to "critical success"
One simply fools the literary press,
But even *they* are rarely taken in
By mediocrities like Trissotin.
How, in another's work, can you condone
Faults that you'd never countenance in your own?
Philaminte You're only seeing faults you want to see,
In view of which we're bound to disagree.

Trissotin enters, carrying a huge rolled-up sheet of paper and some kind of portable stand to display it on

Trissotin It's quite incredible! A friend of mine
At MIT has just been on the line—
Last night all missile stations were alerted—
A holocaust was narrowly averted:
The radar screens picked up a flock of cranes,
Which somebody "mistook" for Russian planes.
The Pentagon's denying it, of course,
But I've no doubts at all about my source.
Philaminte In point of fact, I don't believe we've spent
Nearly enough time on disarmament—
It's of paramount concern to all of us,
And something we should certainly discuss.
Trissotin In the meantime, perhaps you'd like to see
A specimen of concrete poetry
On the subject of this near catastrophe:
It's called "Is It a Plane? Is It a Crane?"

At this point, Trissotin should unfurl and display his poem, which takes the form of an ambiguous shape (plane/crane) defined by repetition of the words "plane" and "crane"

Philaminte Trissotin! You've excelled yourself again!
Trissotin I have to say—I think it's rather fun.
Clitandre Explain it to me.
Trissotin   It's a visual pun ...
Philaminte Don't waste your time on *him*—he's not inclined
To overstretch a rather humdrum mind.
Clitandre That's not quite fair—I'm all for intellect—

It's intellectual posing I reject.
I'd *rather* have no thoughts than rush about
Hawking them, like some intellectual tout.
Trissotin A little learning is a dangerous thing.
Clitandre Learning in any quantity can bring
Disaster in its wake.
Trissotin   I must admit
That's a nice paradox.
Clitandre   It's not a bit
Paradoxical—it's all too commonplace—
In fact, it's staring us right in the face.
Trissotin If *learning's* harmful we don't stand a chance,
When there's already so much ignorance.
Clitandre You're wrong: these gangs of *learned* fools can do
A lot more damage than the ignorant few.
Trissotin Ignorance and folly are synonymous.
Clitandre Not quite—but "fool" and "pedant" are as close
As any two words *can* be.
Trissotin   Folly can't
Be more complete than in the ignorant.
Clitandre But learning in a fool will often add
To the natural folly he already had.
Trissotin You're some advertisement for ignorance!
Clitandre It's thanks to fools like you I take this stance.
Philaminte (*to Clitandre*)
What are you driving at?
Clitandre   Don't help him out—
He's doing well—he's still in with a shout.
Armande This is despicable.
Clitandre (*in mock apology, to Trissotin*)
                    It looks as though
I'm outnumbered—I think I'd better go.
Philaminte I'm not against a frank exchange of views,
But why descend to personal abuse?
Clitandre The man's under perpetual attack—
Abuse! What's that? Water off a duck's back
To him!
Trissotin It comes as no surprise to me
That *you* praise ignorance and stupidity—
You're ambitious and, God knows, the Government's
Full to the brim with ignorant fools.
Clitandre   Nonsense!
The mediocrity's perpetual claim:
Somehow the State has cheated him of fame.
I fear the powers that be are rather more
Discerning than you give them credit for.
Philaminte (*to Clitandre*)
Your attitude's not hard to understand,

Since love and lunacy go hand in hand.

Clitandre is about to refute this as ...

A distraught Vadius enters

Vadius Madame! Trissotin claims he's going to marry
Your daughter. Well, before you let him carry
Her off, I'm here to warn you that his main
Motive is sure to be financial gain:
He's just a money-grubbing charlatan—
How could she spend a lifetime with a man
Like that? There's worse, though—he's a plagiarist too:
A friend of mine's just shown me a review
That blows the lid on him—look, here it is!
(*He attempts to show her a newspaper cutting*)
Philaminte Monsieur, it seems you're in a dreadful tiz.
Vadius It's true, though—scarcely anything he writes
Is really his—he's terminally trite—
An intellectual grave-robber—Foucault,
Derrida, Lacan—they went out years ago.
He even writes concrete poetry.
Clitandre (*indicating the poem which Vadius, in his agitation, has failed to notice*)

                        We know.
Vadius Good God!
Philaminte (*to Vadius*)

                I think perhaps you'd better leave.
Vadius Don't blame me when you find you've been deceived.

Vadius exits, pausing to scrutinize, and spit on, the poem

Trissotin The bastard spat on it!
(*He runs to the door and calls after Vadius*)

                          Trust you to spit
On works of art, you ignorant little shit!!
Philaminte (*to Trissotin*)
These marriage plans of mine appear to have
Stirred up a hornet's nest—wave upon wave
Of pygmies aiming their pathetic darts
At the towering colossus of your art.
This latest outburst only makes me more
Fiercely determined than I was before:
Today, as ever is, I mean to thwart
These jealous fools for good and all—in short,
Tonight you'll be engaged to Henriette.
That'll show Vadius how much store I set
By his opinion. (*To Clitandre*) As for you, monsieur—
I hoped you might agree to be an usher
At my daughter's wedding—you're a family friend—

It's an offer I'm delighted to extend.
Now, Trissotin, you'd better come with me
And help me to devise our strategy.

Philaminte exits, followed by Trissotin

Armande Things aren't too hopeful, from your point of view—
And may I say, my heart goes out to you.
Clitandre The sympathy's a little premature.
Armande You're going to need it soon.
Clitandre   Don't be too sure.
Armande I fear the odds have swung against you, though.
Clitandre Your fears may yet prove groundless, even so.
Armande I hope so.
Clitandre Oh, that's sweet of you.
Armande   And I
Shall do my best—on that you can rely.
Clitandre I'm sure I can—I'm touched by your concern!

Armande exits

Clitandre pours himself a drink

Henriette enters from where Trissotin and Philaminte exited earlier

Henriette Events have taken a distressing turn—
Short of a miracle, it's hard to see
This ending happily for you and me.

Chrysale enters

Chrysale Now then ... (*Seeing the poem*) Good God! What's that?!
Clitandre   A visual
pun.
Chrysale A what?
Clitandre   It's something Trissotin's just done.

Chrysale dons spectacles and approaches the scroll

Chrysale (*reading, as jibberish*) "PLAN-E-CRAN-E-PLAN-E ... "??
Clitandre   It's
meant to be.
"PLANE ... CRANE ... PLANE ... CRANE ..." Got it?!
Chrysale (*mystified*)
                                                        Ah, yes—I
see.
Clitandre *He's marrying Henriette*—or that's the plan.
Chrysale Henriette marry that appalling man!
Philaminte's living in a world of dreams—
Inventing all these dictatorial schemes!
I really think she's gone stark staring mad.
Clitandre That's the effect Trissotin's "Verse" has had.
She's confident of getting her own way.

Chrysale Over my dead body! No—today's the day
When I establish my authority
Once and for all—both of you, follow me.

Chrysale makes a portentous but solitary exit

Henriette They say people are rarely what they seem!
Let's hope it lasts.
Clitandre   Your uncle's got some scheme—
But in the end, who cares if it succeeds—
You say you love me, and that's all I need.
Henriette (*suddenly irritated*)
Of course I love you—are you doubting me?
Clitandre My happiness depends on it, you see.
Henriette But there *are* forces pulling us apart.
Clitandre Well, let them, since you've promised me your heart.
Henriette Vows of undying love are rarely kept—
I haven't *promised* anything, except
That I'll move Heaven and Earth to get my way.

Henriette exits

Clitandre Heaven and Earth are in for quite a day!

Black-out

ACT V

The same

Henriette and Trissotin

Henriette Monsieur: I thought perhaps we might discuss
    This marriage business—just the two of us.
    I felt, in view of all the turmoil here,
    You might just lend a sympathetic ear.
    Whoever gets me gets a fortune too—
    That fact can scarcely have eluded you—
    But shouldn't someone of your cast of mind
    Despise considerations of that kind?
Trissotin I do—it's not your fortune I desire—
    It's you—your beauty's set my heart on fire!
    Your grace and charm are worth any amount
    Of money in a numbered bank account.
Henriette I see. Well, much as I appreciate
    The compliment, I can't reciprocate.
    Although I have a great respect for you,
    I've got one lover and I don't need two.
    Oh, I'm a fool—you're much the worthier man—
    In fact, I'm practically your biggest fan—
    But there it is—my judgement's all askew—
    I love Clitandre—there's nothing I can do.
Trissotin I'm confident that, if you married me,
    You'd fall in love with me eventually.
Henriette Impossible. Clitandre's the only one
    I'm ever going to love—what's done is done:
    Your overtures just make my passion all
    The more erratic and irrational.
    Of course, if people loved by choice, I'm sure
    That *you* would be the one I opted for,
    But, as it is, I feel your wisest move
    Would be to find some other girl to love:
    A man of such considerable . . . parts
    Shouldn't have any trouble winning hearts.
Trissotin What can I do to make you change your mind?
    Set me a task—a mission of some kind—
    But don't expect me to stop loving you,
    Unless you're going to change completely, too.

Henriette No—please don't talk like that—this isn't me—
It's some nymph out of pastoral poetry.
Trissotin My love seems to embarrass you—I fear
There's more embarrassment to come—I'm here
To stay: it's part of my philosophy
To relish, and defeat, adversity:
I'll take whatever you can throw at me.
Henriette Well! I'm impressed. In fact, I don't deserve
A husband of such calibre, such nerve!
You need a woman who not only sees,
But compliments your many qualities—
How could a man like you possibly be
Interested in an idiot like me?
Trissotin I'm not discouraged by a little stalling.
Philaminte (*off*) Trissotin!
Trissotin   I must go—your mother's calling.

Trissotin exits and Chrysale enters

Chrysale Ah, there you are—it's time for Operation
Male Dominance—all hands to battle stations!
Henriette Still in this strangely warlike frame of mind!
Just keep it up—if anyone can find
Your weak spot *she* can. (*She gestures off to an absent Philaminte*)
Chrysale   Am I such a clot?
Am I a milksop?
Henriette   No. Of course you're not.
Chrysale I'm not retarded—I can form a plan
And act on it, like any rational man.
Henriette I know you can.
Chrysale   I may be getting old
But I can still control my own household.
Henriette Certainly.
Chrysale   I refuse to spend my life
Just playing second fiddle to my wife.
Henriette About time, too.
Chrysale   What are you driving at?
Why did you try to slap me down like that?!
Henriette I *wasn't* trying to slap you down!
Chrysale   I'll show
That bullying bitch who's boss round here.
Henriette   Bravo!
Chrysale I thought I'd open the hostilities
By bringing back Martine.
Henriette   A fiendish wheeze!

Martine enters

Martine I'm right be'ind you—don't you worry now—
We're gonna crucify that bossy cow!!

Clitandre enters

Clitandre Sorry I'm late.
Chrysale   All right, then—we're a quorum.
My brother's busy, but we're ready for 'em.

Noises, off

Henriette We'll soon see—I can hear them coming down.
Chrysale Oh God! Hold fast! Everyone rally round!

Philaminte enters, followed by Trissotin

Philaminte (*seeing Martine*)
Martine! Why are you here?
(*Turning on Chrysale*)
                                                    Kindly explain
Why this imbecile is in my house again.
Chrysale We can discuss such minor points as that as
Time allows, but there *are* more pressing matters.
Philaminte Then I assume you haven't given in?
Chrysale No. Henriette's not marrying Trissotin
She doesn't want to—and besides, it's plain
He's only in this for financial gain.
Philaminte Financial gain, indeed! That's very funny.
As if a man like him cares about money.
Chrysale Money or no money, I'm telling you:
HENRIETTE'S MARRYING CLITANDRE.
Philaminte   Says who?
Chrysale SAYS ME.
Martine I know it's none of my business 'n all that, but if yer want my view,
An 'usband's word is final.
Chrysale   Very true.
Martine Let me tell you, I've worked in quite a lot er really 'igh-class 'ouses
In my time, and I don't think I ever seen a wife what wore the trousers.
Chrysale Well said.
Martine   What's more, when the 'usband—'ow shall I put it—
wears the frock,
As you might say, 'e's gen'rally a complete 'n utter larfin' stock.
Chrysale (*rueful*)
How true that is!
Martine   If I 'ad an 'usband I'd tell 'im straight—I'd say:
"Look, mate, I absolutely bloody insist on you 'avin yer own way,
Got it? If I ever does anythink what you don't like, like prattlin' on 'n so
forth, like I tend to—you got an 'and—
Use it! I mean belt me one! Understand?"
Chrysale Come, come!
Martine   I mean it. 'n anyway, why should Henriette marry a
jumped-up, arty-farty little git like Monsieur Trissotin,
When there's Monsieur Clitandre, what loves 'er—'n's such an 'an'some
charmin' man?

Chrysale My sentiments exactly.
Philaminte   Has she quite
 Finished?
Martine   I mean to say, it wouldn' be right
 to fob 'er off with a weed what's got 'is 'ead
 Full er books 'n stuff, and probably ain't no good in bed.
 I won' say another word.

A pause during which Philaminte attempts to speak

                              But if you ask me,
 The ideal 'usband wouldn' even know 'is friggin' ABC!

Before Philaminte can turn on her, Martine makes a haughty exit

Philaminte Your spokesperson's highly articulate.
Chrysale I endorse her every word.
Philaminte   Now, let me state
 My own position: briefly, either she
 Marries Trissotin, or lives in poverty.
 That's how it's going to be—as for Clitandre—
 If he wants to marry, he can have Armande.
Chrysale (*pausing for a moment to work it out*)
 That's quite a good idea! (*To Henriette*) What do you say?
 You marry him—he marries her.
Clitandre ⎫ (*together*)   NO WAY!!!
Henriette ⎭

*At this point the telephone rings. Chrysale answers it. From his responses it is
clear that some grave news is being communicated*

 During the following, Bélise enters

Trissotin (*to Henriette*)
 Give me a chance—I know you won't regret it.
 I'll dedicate my books to you ...
Henriette   Forget it.

Bélise takes, or rather drags, Clitandre to one side

Bélise I hope you're coming round tonight.
Clitandre   Oh, no!
Bélise Dinner for two ... and after ...
Clitandre   Let me go!
Bélise You really put my patience to the test.
Clitandre I've had enough of this—it's quite grotesque!
 (*He breaks away from her and rejoins Henriette*)
 Marry me anyway—let's stay together—
 My flat's not up to much, but we could ...
Henriette   Never!
 My bedroom's bigger than that flat of yours.
 We've got to do it *my* way.
Clitandre   Why?

Henriette   Because.
Chrysale (*returning from the phone; to Philaminte, smouldering*)
    That play you backed, by some "expressionist" freak—
    The one that folded in its second week ...
Philaminte Well? What about it?
Chrysale   Did you see the budget?
Philaminte I may have done.
Chrysale   But DID YOU??!!
Philaminte   Budget, smudgeit—
    It was a brilliant play—extremely funny—
    To hell with critics (*an apologetic glance at Trissotin*) and to hell with
    money.
Chrysale You're liable for quite a large amount—
    It's half a million francs, at the last count.
Philaminte Who cares? As far as I'm concerned, this loss
    Is insignificant—just so much dross.

*The telephone rings again. Chrysale answers, this time handing it to Phila-
minte. Her reactions indicate genuine, if frenzied, delight*

Trissotin (*portentous, as usual*)
    That play—it could have been a brilliant work ...
Clitandre If it hadn't been written by a brainless burk?
Trissotin That's just the sort of ignorant attack
    You get from someone——
Clitandre   —who despises hacks.
Philaminte (*returning from the phone, triumphant; to Chrysale*)
    Remember that investment banker ponce
    Who sold you an office block in la Défense?
Chrysale What of it?
Philaminte We've been well and truly rooked.
Chrysale How do you mean?
Henriette   Our lawyers overlooked
    One tiny fact—it wasn't his to sell,
    Which means, of course, it's not ours either.
Chrysale   Well?
    We'll get our money back? Won't we?
Philaminte   We might ...
    The ponce in question disappeared last night.
Chrysale He can't have done! This might mean bankruptcy!
Philaminte Bankrupt or rich—it's all the same to me:
    Civilized people welcome shocks like these—
    They strip us bare, and help us find true peace
    Of mind. Stop making this disgraceful fuss!

By now Chrysale is virtually in tears

    Trissotin, tell him you'll look after us.
Trissotin Actually I've been thinking—since it's clear
    I'm not exactly popular round here,

Perhaps it might be better if we let
The matter drop.
Philaminte   But why? You've hardly set
Much store by *that* objection up to now.
Trissotin Perhaps I haven't—but I don't see how
I'm ever going to find a way to make
Her love me—let's just call it a mistake.
Philaminte But this is just preposterous! Was I wrong
To like you and admire you for so long?
Trissotin Think what you like—it doesn't interest me—
Just put it down to mediocrity—
But I'm afraid you really must excuse me
If I don't stay to hear you all abuse me!

Trissotin flounces out, bumping into Armande as she enters

Armande What's going on?
Henriette   Trissotin's done a bunk.
Bélise It's terrible—I thought he had more spunk!
Philaminte He's nothing but a pompous, puffed-up, crass,
      Mercenary, talentless, conceited ass!
Clitandre Do me the honour of allowing me
      To take my share of this calamity.
      I'm scarcely rich, but I'll do all I can
      To help . . .
Philaminte   Now, there's a truly generous man!
      I'm proud to have you for a son-in-law—
      God knows what my objections were before!
Henriette I hate to disobey you yet again,
      But I'm afraid I can't accept him . . .
Clitandre   When
      The major obstacle has been removed?!
Henriette The situation's changed . . .
Clitandre   Yes—it's improved!
Henriette Not so: I dreamed of putting your affairs
      To rights—not loading you with extra cares—
      I love you far too much to marry you.
Clitandre But any hardship's well-worth going through
      To keep your love.
Henriette   I think we ought to part—
      That's not your reason talking, it's your heart,
      And if you marry me you'll soon agree
      That love's no antidote to poverty.
      No—if you really love me, go away:
      You'll only start to hate me if you stay.

Ariste enters

Chrysale (*to Ariste*)
      She's turned him down!

Ariste   No! Why?
Chrysale   Because we're poor.
Ariste (*mischievously*)
  Really?! Since when?
Chrysale (*looking at his watch*)
                            Since about half-past four.
Ariste (*to Henriette*)
  And this is all that's making you refuse?
Henriette Of course.
Ariste   I think it's time to disabuse
  You all—those phone calls, they were just a ruse
  To expose Trissotin for what he was—
  Naughty of me—but all in a good cause!

Chrysale hugs Ariste hysterically

Philaminte Won't Trissotin be flabbergasted, though,
  When we announce it in *Le Figaro*!
Bélise It serves him right for being such a fraud.
Armande As usual *I've* been totally ignored!
Philaminte Use your philosophy, and be content—
  This is a time for general merriment.
Bélise (*to the lovers*)
  Be careful, though—this step may prove a rash one—
  The embers of Clitandre's former passion
  May yet flare up again . . .
Henriette (*to Clitandre*)   What passion's that?!

Clitandre can only shrug

Bélise Didn't you know? He *was* my lover . . .
Henriette ⎫
Armande ⎬ (*together*)   WHAT?!
Philaminte ⎭
Chrysale Never mind her—a wedding's what we need,
  And quickly, too. (*To Philaminte, pleading*) Agreed?
Rest, bar Armande   Agreed?
Philaminte   Agreed.

Black-out

FURNITURE AND PROPERTY LIST

We list below only essential items of furniture as mentioned in the text. Further dressing may be added at the director's discretion.

ACT I

On stage: Table. *On it:* drinks, glasses
Telephone

Off stage: Nil

Personal: **Bélise:** wrist-watch (required throughout)
Chrysale: wrist-watch (required throughout)

ACT II

On stage: As Act I

Off stage: Nil

ACT III

On stage: As Act I

Off stage: Manuscript **(Trissotin)**

Personal: **Trissotin:** manuscript in pocket
Vadius: manuscript in pocket

ACT IV

On stage: As Act I

Off stage: Sheet of paper and portable stand **(Trissotin)**
Newspaper cutting **(Vadius)**

Personal: **Chrysale:** glasses in pocket

ACT V

On stage: As Act I

Off stage: Nil

LIGHTING PLOT

Property fittings required: *nil*

Interior. A salon. The same scene throughout

ACT I

To open: Full general lighting

Cue 1   **Clitandre:** "... have to do to get it!"   (Page 8)
          Black-out

ACT II

To open: Full general lighting

Cue 2   **Chrysale:** "My very sexuality's at stake!"   (Page 17)
          Black-out

ACT III

To open: Full general lighting

Cue 3   **Chrysale** wanders off and the lovers continue their embrace   (Page 28)
          Black-out

ACT IV

To open: Full general lighting

Cue 4   **Clitandre:** "... are in for quite a day!"   (Page 35)
          Black-out

ACT V

To open: Full general lighting

Cue 5   **Philaminte:** "Agreed."   (Page 42)
          Black-out

EFFECTS PLOT

ACT I

No cues

ACT II

No cues

ACT III

No cues

ACT IV

No cues

ACT V

Cue 1   **Chrysale:** "... but we're ready for 'em."   (Page 38)
         Noises, off

Cue 2   **Clitandre** and **Henriette:** "NO WAY!!!"   (Page 39)
         Telephone rings

Cue 3   **Philaminte:** "Is insignificant—just so much dross."   (Page 40)
         Telephone rings

MADE AND PRINTED IN GREAT BRITAIN BY
LATIMER TREND & COMPANY LTD PLYMOUTH
MADE IN ENGLAND